THE MAKING OF A WOMAN

OVERCOMING EVERY OBSTACLE
OBTAINING VICTORY

BY LISA A. BROWN

The Making of a Woman

LISA A. BROWN, 2015 -
THE MAKING OF A WOMAN
OVERCOMING EVERY OBSTACLE
OBTAINING VICTORY: Experiments ● Analogies ● Quotes ● Case studies ●Testimonies ●Affirmations ● A Tool Box Kit ● *My Story*

Includes: bibliographical sources, scriptures meditations, answers quiz

CASE STUDY HAS SOME DRAMATIZE
Copyright © 2015 by Lisa A. Brown

All rights reserved. No part of this book may be reproduced by any mechanical, photographic, or electronic process, or electronic process, or in the form of a phonographic recording, nor may it be stored in a retrieval system, transmitted, or otherwise be copied for public or private use- other than for "Fair use" as brief quotations embodied in articles and reviews without prior written permission of the publisher.

Library of Congress Catalog Number 2015904769

ISBN 978-0-692-54514-0

Publisher: Shine4 Jesus

All Biblical Quotes are from the King James Version unless otherwise stated.

Dedication

May this book help you to understand and trust the divine process, plan, and purpose of the Creator. May you become a Vessel of Honor, power, strength, value, courage, integrity, wealth, longevity, and excellence as *you overcome every obstacle that come your way.*

The Making of a Woman

Acknowledgments

I acknowledge with great love, faith and honor:

>Pierre, Dominika, Genesis, Samaria, and Remiah. My grandchildren, Pierre Jr., PreAnna, Gemma, Matthew, Tiffany, Donnie and Regina.
>
>My congregation at *Walking in the Shekinah Glory Global Ministry*.
>
>My team at *Rainbow Covenant Economic Development Center* who shares the dream of helping me to aid in combating poverty and injustice while promoting prosperity and justice through education, empowering and encouraging classes and *change* meetings -- all to break the cycle of despair and to help individuals discover their God-given gifts and talents.
>
>All my Clients from *WDI? J & A New U! Salon and* all those whose hearts are willing to trust God each and every day through the process.
>
> *Lisa A. Brown*

Contents

Dedication
Acknowledgement

Part One

Piece 1	Arise and Shine……………………………….....7
Piece 2	Two Perspectives………………................……11
Piece 3	Inspirational & Motivational Tips…………..…15
Piece 4	Experiment and Analogy………..………..……17
Piece 5	Intro/Obstacle Quiz………....……………..……21
Piece 6	Definitions ……………………………….……25
Piece 7	Inspirational & Motivational Tips……………..29
Piece 8	Body, Soul & Spirit ……………….….…………33

Part Two

Piece 9	Analogy #2: Potter-Clay …………....….…...39
Piece 10	Helen Keller ……………………...………… 45
Piece 11	Rose Kennedy……………………………..…51
Piece 12	Madam CJ Walker …………………....………57

Part Three

Piece 13	Body Testimony 1…………………………....……61
Piece 14	Soul Testimony 2……..……………..………..69
Piece 15	Spirit Testimony 3……………………...…..…...75

Part Four

Piece 16	Ruth Modeling …………………...………….79
Piece 17	Vision……………………………………...…..81
Piece 18	40 Day Power Pack Plan……………………...83
Piece 19	What do you see?……………….……………....87
Piece 20	My Story……………………………….......91

Scripture Meditation for a New Perspective (97)
Answer Key (100)
Reference   (101)

The Making of a Woman

Never, Never, Never give up nor in on your Greatness!

~ *For we are God's Masterpiece* ~

Everything will fall into place…

Life is like a big puzzle. Though our futures may not be clear or turn out exactly as we expected. Each of us has the strength inside to put the puzzle together ~ we just have to look for the right pieces.

At times, it will appear to be impossible, but you must keep believing. Life's pieces have a way of coming together when you least expect it. – Renee M. Betalik

Piece 1

Arise and Shine

Let your light so shine before men, that they may see your good works, and glorify your Father which is in heaven.
-Matthews 5:16

"IT IS BETTER TO LIGHT A CANDLE THAN CURSE THE DARKNESS."
-ELEANOR ROOSEVELT

I affirm that I was made to Rise and Shine in the darkness!

The Making of a Woman

Recently I turned on my computer to see horrifying news. An earthquake had killed 8,000 and affected over 8 million people. In another story, a riot broke out in Boston when people reacted to alleged injustice within a local correctional center when a prisoner died while in police custody. Many people were severely hurt and over 200 arrests were made and just when you think that it can't get any worse: A former U.S. Olympic Gold Medal winner streamed crossed the internet declaring he is transforming from a man into a woman because he really feels like a woman in his soul. Not to mention, he has six children and has been married three times. Shockingly, many seemed to think nothing is morally wrong or abnormal about this kind of behavior. However, in contrast, twenty Ethiopian Christians were murder execution style by Islamic militants in Libya. Horrible news indeed.

Today, you must have a made-up mind to shine and to become who the Creator predestined you to be. *Only the maker of a thing knows its true objective, purpose or potential.* America has forgotten her Maker and now is the time we must be armed with the Truth that is, information and the inspiration to bring about true transformation to overcome any and every obstacle.

To impact our world for Good, we must Arise and Shine!

Women! God wants you to ARISE and SHINE in the midst of the darkness. That's right you are commanded to SHINE! How do you do that? By fulfilling your God given purpose and by embracing your life work with all your heart, soul, and might! That's right you and I have a job to do; a life assignment that is revealed day by day.

The Bible speaks of these dark days in Isaiah 60:1-2, *"Arise [from the depression and prostration in which circumstances have kept you—rise to a new life]! Shine (be radiant with the glory of the Lord), for your light has come, and the glory of the Lord has risen upon you!* [2] *For behold, darkness shall cover the earth, and dense darkness [all] peoples, but the Lord shall arise upon you [O Jerusalem], and His glory shall be seen on you.* [3] *And nations shall come to your light, and kings to the brightness of your rising."*

This book in no way is meant to be the total answer for reaching your full potential. My prayer is that Our Maker would use this book to strengthen you so that you can overcome ever obstacle that comes your way. How?

Through gaining insight on how our Maker can use difficulties, hardships, devastations, calamities, death, abandonment, and misfortunes to reveal our true life work!

The Making of a Woman

To aid you in this endeavor, this book contains:
Experiments ● Analogies ● Quotes ● Case studies
●Testimonies ●Affirmations ● A Tool Box Kit ● *My Story*

I confess that my strength rises in the day of adversity, that's when I am at my best.

Robert Schuller said, *"Tough times don't last, but tough people do."*

Therefore, I confess, that I am tougher and stronger than life or my circumstances.

Piece 2

Two Perspectives

The Cat represents the natural realm and the Lion represents the spirit realm that is your true potential

There are two realms that coexist at the same time, the natural realm and the spiritual realm. The natural realm or also called the physical realm deals with what you can see, touch, taste, feel, and hear: the five senses. The spiritual realm deals with what you cannot see naturally, the non-physical things, but you can see and feel the effects of it. For example, the wind, you cannot see it however you can see and feel the effects of it, (e.g. objects blowing in the air).

Both realms will affect how you see and what you see. We must acknowledge both realms exist because when our true potential is [1]unlocked we will understand and overcome the limitations that exist in the natural realm.

---

[1]*Pray unlock my true potential ~*

The Making of a Woman

Remember what we said about the wind? The spirit realm is that realm you cannot see however you can see and feel the effects of it. What we believe, think, say and do, can manifest in our "seen" realm.

If you believe you can, you can but if you believe that you can't then you can't.

Remember the story of a little engine train: A long train must be pulled over a high mountain. Larger engines treated anthropomorphically (liken to human strength), are asked to pull the train; for various reasons they refuse. The request is sent to a small engine, who agrees to try. The engine succeeds in pulling the train over the mountain while repeating: "I-think-I-can, I-think-I-can".

The principal theme *a stranded train is unable to find an engine willing to take it on over difficult terrain to its destination that was capable, however they were unwilling to entertain the thoughts that they could. Only the little engine is willing to try and, while repeating the mantra "I think I can, I think I can"* overcomes a seemingly impossible task.

Daily Affirmations, positive self-talk, confessions and visualization will help you do the impossible and overcome insurmountable obstacles.

The children's story outlined above in the *Little Engine That Could* is actually a pretty accurate model for what works in our everyday life.

Researchers at Kent's School of Sport and Exercise Science in Ohio, picked 46 studies out of thousands on the efficacy of psychological interventions on endurance athletes. The study concluded that athletes who kept a positive outlook and had daily affirmations showed a higher degree of success – the conclusion, positive self-talk and visualization works!

"As he calculates the cost to himself, this is what he does"
Proverbs 23:7 - *GWV*

"For as he thinketh in his heart, so is he"
Proverbs 23:7 - *KJV*

The Making of a Woman

Lessons:

- I live in two realms. The natural realm has many limitations but the spiritual realm is where my true potential is realized.
- The spiritual realm effects how and what I see, how I respond determines the end result in the natural realm.
- My perspective creates my reality

Principle:

The power of thinking and seeing releases unlimited possibilities.

Fill in the blank: I think I can

_____

_____

_____

_____

_____

_____

_____

_____

Piece 3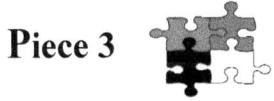

Inspirational & Motivational Tips

~ Everything that is was made first ~
- Lisa A. Brown

You can live and finish up strong with much insight! You must believe that you can make it and then go for it! Everything that exists had to be made first: cars, cakes, table, house, and even you! The maker of the car, cake, table, house, and you . . . knows the original purpose and use for the thing they make.

You were made and formed by God. God made you for a particular purpose. I challenge you to gain a whole new perspective concerning everyday living and the obstacles facing you right now or that you will face in the future.

You will discover that every obstacle is an opportunity for you to discover your true potential and to fulfill your intended purpose by your MAKER for your MAKING! You can get excited because GOD is about to propel and strengthen you to walk in your purpose!!!

"The impediment to action advances action. What stands in the way becomes the way." — Marcus Aurelius

The Making of a Woman

Harriet Tubman was a slave who became famous because she freed thousands of slaves by the Underground Railroad. She turned all the obstacles she faced in freeing the slaves into a gateway opportunity. Ms. Tubman had a plan. She befriended many southern whites who were sympathetic to the plight of slaves along with many black freemen. When they all came together, they helped countless slaves to escape under very dangerous conditions and routes. In conclusion, Harriet Tubman used enormous obstacles to help thousands to achieve freedom from oppression.

Lessons:

- You can do the impossible with strong determination.
- What I see was made twice: first in my mind and second in the natural realm where I can see, touch, and feel.
- What is in the way, becomes the way.

Principle:

- Every obstacle you face is full of opportunity.

Fill in the blank: What obstacle(s) am I facing?

_____

_____

Can you think of any opportunities that could possible exist in your obstacles: Can the obstacle help you to gain wisdom, strength, or patience?

Piece 4

Experiment and Analogy

Now let's explore Parts versus Whole: Let's make a cake!

Let's conduct an experiment. Before making a cake, set out each one of the ingredients on your cooking space. Now we are going to do something different. We are going to taste each individual ingredient found in a chocolate cake first, before putting it all together. Think about it. Have you ever tasted baking powder? How about baking soda? The flour is horribly bland and what about a raw egg? Even the "semi-sweet" chocolate taste terribly bitter compared to the sweet milk chocolate taste of the finished cake. To sum it up, *almost everything that goes into this cake tastes absolutely terrible by itself.*

The phenomenal event takes place when all the ingredients are mixed together in the right amounts. An amazing metamorphosis takes place -- a delicious edible cake! ....While the individual ingredients taste bitter or terrible, the final product taste terrific! If I had judged the whole cake on the basis of the individual ingredients, I would never believe it would taste so good.

Here's the point, the individual ingredients of trials and apparent tragedies in our lives are neither "delicious" nor desirable. In fact, they are often very bland or even bitter. But God, *shall I call Him the Master Baker?* is capable of carefully measuring out and mixing up all your

The Making of a Woman

Experiences or ingredients in order to produce a final product that is truly good. He does not ask us to immediately see that every individual event is wonderful. But He does expect us to trust that He is sovereignly at work and will use the event along with everything else for our very best good (Alcom, 2010).

Insight: Our trials, tribulations, and obstacles could be viewed as *the making of a wonderfully delicious cake:* each ingredient or experience has been combined to make us *wonderfully* made. It depends on your perspective!

Think on the scripture, *"And we know that all things worked together for good to them that love God, to them who are called according to his purpose"*. Romans 8:28

Lessons:

- When we look at a part without considering the whole, brokenness is inevitable.
- Remember the Maker is up to something GOOD in your life.
- With the right perspective, what comes in our lives to break us can actually MAKE us!

Principle:

- All things are working together for your GOOD and the good of others!

Fill in the Blanks:

Can you identify some painful moments in your life that if you put them all together they would begin to make sense or reveal your life's purpose? *Take a few minutes and really do some deep reflecting.* Look back and connect the dots.

_____
_____
_____

_____

Can you also identify where those past challenges, pains, or difficulties continue to show up in your new relationships, e.g. lack of trust and fearful of being hurt?

_____
_____

The Making of a Woman

_____
_____

What did you discover? Do those past hurts and challenges, hurt or help you in your present circumstances?

_____
_____
_____
_____

Good news!
You can TRUST your MAKER that He knows what He is doing!

Piece 5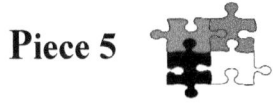

Intro/Obstacle Quiz

Nothing happens to anybody which he is not fitted by nature to bear. - Marcus Aurelius

Do you feel like something is holding you back? Is there something blocking your path in life?

If so, it could be an obstacle. Obstacles come in all different shapes and sizes. Identifying the obstacles you face helps you to learn how to deal with them and how to keep from making the same mistakes over and over again.

It may sound strange, but your attitude and perception is key to overcoming any obstacle.

Nothing is an obstacle when you view everything that happens, as an opportunity and a tool.

The next page is a quick quiz with a list of 12 different types of obstacles you may be facing in your life.

The Making of a Woman

What Kind of Obstacle Is It?

1. Bars 2. Blocks 3. Challenges 4. Checks 5. Dampers
6. Hurdles 7. Impassable Obstacles 8. Impediments
9. Knots 10. Turnstiles 11. Vices 12. Walls

Below are twelve definitions of different obstacles. Can you identify and define each obstacle? Place a number next to the definition that you believe matches the right description.

Let's do the first one together . . .

    A. __12__ makes you look around for a ladder or an overhanging tree you can climb. Or they can inspire you to build a ramp so everyone can climb over them.

A wall would make you look around for a ladder to climb or build a ramp to get over it.

    B. _____ helps you to stretch and become more flexible, just like a dancer uses to warm-up.

    C. _____ Helps you bide your time until things change.

    D. _____ makes you stop and look carefully at the way things are connected and then works patiently to loosen or cut through the binds within yourself or your environment.

    E. _____ puts the pressure on and tests whether we are strong enough to handle the consequences.

F. _____ forces you to find another way around them.

G. _____ helps you slow down and exercise caution in choosing your next steps.

H. _____ makes it necessary to reposition yourself for a new start, in the same way that runners use ___ before they start a race.

I. _____ helps you grow your knowledge, skills, experience and resources.

J. _____ requires you to gain momentum so you can leap over them.

K. _____ helps you slow down and cool off, just like a fireplace damper.

L. _____ makes you to rethink your options and actions, in the same way a check in the game of chess does.

Answer key on page 98

Knowing the nature of what is holding you back and the means by which it does -- is critical to choosing the right strategy to deal with it. ~Anonymous

The Making of a Woman

What are some of your obstacles?

Mentally_____
_____
_____
_____

Emotionally_____
_____
_____
_____
_____

Financially_____
_____
_____
_____
_____

Physically_____
_____
_____
_____

Spiritually_____
_____
_____
_____

Piece 6

Definitions

Obstacles must be O-V-E-R-C-O-M-E to obtain victory. You cannot obtain victory if you are not willing to be [2]M- A-D-E. There is always a Making first.

Definitions:

Making –The act of one that makes: similar to the **making** of a cake analogy I used in the earlier chapter. It is the process of creating, forming or putting together. To bring into being, build, or create. The process of coming into being - *Synonym*: molding.

Before we can shine in the midst of the darkness we must learn how to overcome our obstacles. What is an obstacle? An obstacle is anything or person that is hindering you from doing what you were created to do. Let's define obstacle.

Obstacle – Something that makes it difficult to do something else. An object that you have to go around or over: something that blocks your path.

Michael Jordon took it even further, he said *"Obstacles don't have to stop you. If you run into a wall, don't turn around and give up. Figure out how to climb it, go through it, or work around it."*

---

[2] *Pray Make me Lord ~*

The Making of a Woman

Obstacles such as depression, fear, bitterness, abandonment, death, racism, low self-esteem, addictions, poverty, chronic exhaustion, death of a love one failure can be OVERCOME.

Say this out loud: *I am an OVERCOMER! I can overcome any and every obstacle that has come my way, that is in my way, or will come my way, I am an Overcomer!*

Overcoming – To defeat someone or something, to successfully deal with or gain control of something difficult. Overcome weakness. To prevail over. To conquer. To get the better of in a struggle or conflict.

Obtain –To gain, acquire or get, to continue to be accepted in use. *Synonym*s: acquire, secure, procure, and come into the passion of. Pick up.

Victory – Success in defeating an opponent or enemy.

The assignment to write this book was given to me over twenty years ago. Was it procrastination, fear, busyness, life calamities, or just God's timing at work in my life to cause this work to be manifested today?

Personally, I have learned a lot walking with the Lord. I have discovered He has a Sovereign plan at work in my life, in the lives of His people, and He uses every experience along the way—no experience or event has been wasted in my life, or yours. Just like when he told his disciples to gather the fragments after he fed the multitudes with the two fishes and five loaves of bread. What look like wasted and useless time; the Creator was shaping and molding me for my intended purpose.

For those who will dare to trust God in their darkest hours, or when it looks like nothing is happening. Just look ahead of you and God will provide just enough light for the step you are on.

It's your time to shine as never before, so shine!

How do I shine? If you hold on in the midst of the darkness and be strong (work……. continue to do good, in the midst of the storm) – you will see that God was at work all the time getting you ready for your purpose and life work!

Let your light so shine before men, that they may see your good works, and glorify your Father which is in heaven – Matthew 5:16

The Making of a Woman

Lessons:

- Obstacles must be overcome
- We are overcomers
- God waste nothing even the fragmented times in our lives.

Principle:

- In the darkest times of our lives, God will provide enough light for the step that we are on.

Fill in the blanks:

I desire to:

_____
_____
_____
_____

Can you name a few obstacles that are holding you back? List them:

_____
_____
_____

How can I shine? E.g. Who can I help? What can I do? What can I give?

_____
_____
_____

Piece 7

Inspirational & Motivational Tips

Live like you were dying and die like you want to live forever – Lisa A. Brown

You can make it through anything with insight! Just believe this truth. Your Maker made you with the ability to overcome and get through it!!! (Whatever the "it" is). Just get up, get out and get **BUSY**! That's right I said, get **Busy**! It's never too late to live and embrace each and every moment as though it is your last. You must begin to live like you are dying and die like you want to live. Looking at life from another perspective ~

"Somebody should tell us, right at the start of our lives that we are dying. Then we might live life to the limit, every minute of every day. Do it! I say. Whatever you want to do, do it now! There are only so many tomorrows."
– Pope Paul VI

How do you live like you are dying and die like you want to live?

Do It Now! – There is no better time than the present. Are there things you have been thinking of doing? Take a few moments . . . Name them out loud one by one. **Now turn that list into opportunities**!

The Making of a Woman

Seize the Opportunity – Opportunities are those things that may present themselves as once in a lifetime event or they may present themselves as tasks with a very small window of time to complete. As a pastor, I have observed those close to death readily admit if they could live their lives over, they would have taken more risks. They wished they would have taken the opportunity when it presented itself instead playing it "safe".

Never Give Up! – Thomas Edison serves as a good example of someone that did not quit. After 1000 attempts he finally created the light bulb. He never gave up.

"Our greatest weakness lies in giving up. The most certain way to succeed is always to try just one more time." – Thomas Edison

Consider Long-Term Consequences – When you evaluate whether to take certain opportunities, look at the big picture versus the little picture, why? Because you must first balance and weigh the risks and the benefits. If the benefits outweigh the risks, greater the guaranteed success.

No one knows when he or she will die so therefore you need to get busy living life on purpose.

Know Yourself – be honest, list and become aware of your weaknesses and your strengths: mentally, emotionally, physically or financially.

Man know thyself: then thou shalt know the Universe and God. – Pythagoras

The power in *living life like you are dying and die like you want to live* enables you to cherish every moment of life and not to just exist or sit back and become complacent.

Seize and live in the moment! On another note, *living like we are dying* also gives us you the will to rise and shine in the midst of a dark and troubled world and embrace your intended purpose.

As stated earlier, for those who will dare to trust God in their darkest hour when you can't see your way out, just look ahead, HOLD ON and don't give up, God will provide just enough light for the step that you are on and you will see that God was at work all the time!

I affirm that I am Strong, when everything is falling apart ~

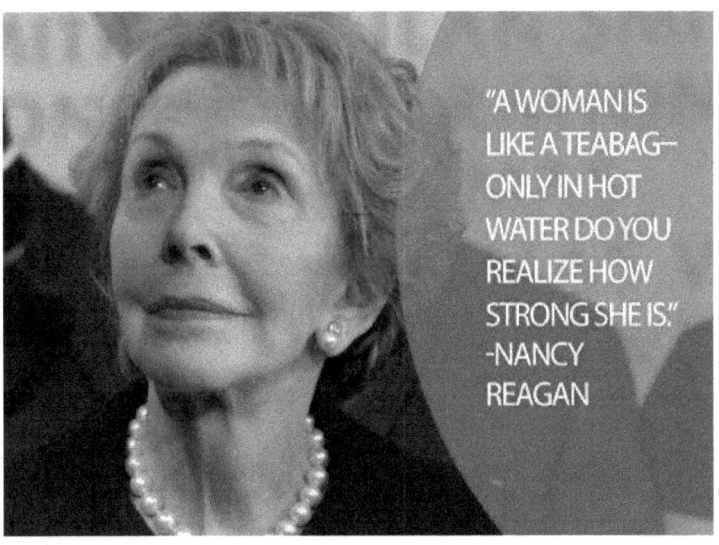

I affirm I am strong when I feel weak ~

31

The Making of a Woman

I affirm that I am becoming stronger and stronger day by day ~

Where do I go from here?
_____
_____
_____

What opportunity (ies) do I need to seize right now?
_____
_____
_____

Complete the rest of this sentence . . . I will never give up_____
_____
_____
_____

If I had a better perspective, what present issue or obstacle could work to my advantage?
_____
_____
_____
_____

Piece 8

We live in a body, we possess a soul, and we are a spirit.

Discovering and fulfilling your life work and reaching your full potential begins with acknowledging that you are a wonderful three-part being made up of a body, soul (mind, will and emotions) and a spirit. These 3-parts are called a *triune*.

You must be clear about your triune composition, that is, you live in a body, you possess a soul and you are a spirit.

We must deal with every individual part of us in order to overcome every obstacle and to engage in meaningful change. To define triune, we will start with part one the body. The body is the "outer covering" or "the house" that stores the soul and spirit. The outer body is in touch with the physical world, it is the part that everyone sees.

Second part is the soul. The soul is comprised of the mind, will and emotions. The mind is the part or the place where thoughts are contemplated before they become actions. The other part of the soul is the will. This is the dynamo of our being. That is our sheer desire to get something done, it defines our will. Just like the story, *The Little Engine That Could*, our will acts as the catalyst and strength to do what is necessary to get what we desire.

The Making of a Woman

The soul is where all emotions (e.g. happy, sad, anger, unforgiveness etc.) or Soul ties exists. *The state of our soul will show up in your everyday choices, in our word usage and how one feel and what a person do.*

The third part is the spirit, it is the <u>real</u> you, also known as the *human spirit*. The human spirit will always allow you to do some amazing things, it is the God in you, when it is awaken by the Holy Spirit (that is another teaching)! This is the part of you, that exist that has never been hurt, or damaged, once you find this place within you, you have discovered your true power, identity, or higher self!

The Bible says that we have this treasure in earthen vessels, that the excellency of the power may be of God, and not of us. 2 Corinthians 4:7

*(1 Thessalonians 5:23, Genesis 1:26, Genesis 2:7
1 Corinthians 9:27)*

To better understand the 3-part triune, this illustration will help you on the next page:

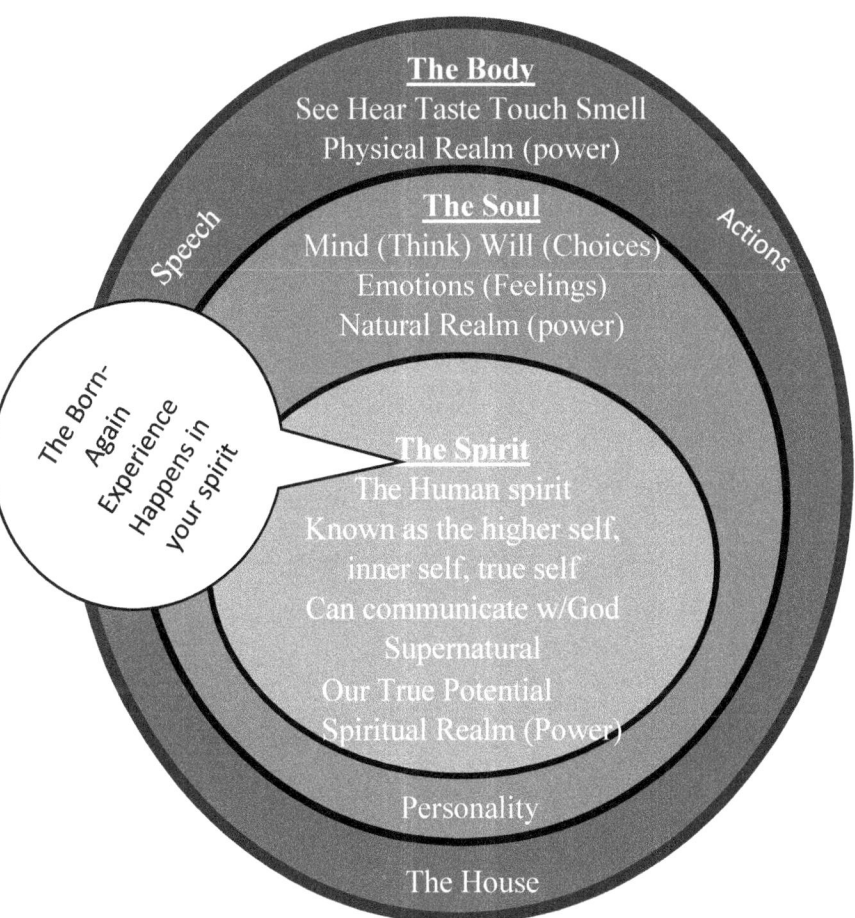

We must understand that we are three-part and as each part plays a role in our overall being, we can be triumphant over our obstacles each and every time! This is why, Nick Vujicic, a Christian motivational speaker who has no arms and no legs can say, "I have no worries." Nick has truly found his power living from the inside out. That is, Nick lives out of his human spirit—the spirit that comes from God.

The Making of a Woman

Fill in the blanks:

I live in a:

_____

I possess a:

_____

I am a:

_____

The body contains: _____

_____

The soul contains: _____

_____

The human spirit contains:

_____

_____

_____

Lesson:
- Our lives must become centered and balanced if we are going to shine in the midst of the darkness through our life work, we are overcomers.

Principle:
- I was built to be triumphant every time!

I affirm that I am willing to be made, to become a Vessel of Honor!

I confess I will never prefer someone else's life or essence over my own unique, special, and powerful essence. I confess, I love me. ~ Lisa A. Brown

Personal Testimony: I remember one of the darkest times in my life, when I was abandon by my husband after sixteen years of marriage. This affirmation brought restoration to me as a whole. I would repeat this affirmation over three hundred times, right before I went to sleep. I would say God loves me, and I love me, another one I would say, God accepts me, and I accept me. You will be surprise of what healing that takes place when we begin to think and speak the right words to ourselves.

Miracle Work and words

God Loves Me, and I Love Me

God Accepts Me, and I Accept Me

Piece 9

Analogy #2
The Art of Making Pottery

Earlier we baked a cake now, let's look at making pottery to illustrate that we are being formed and shaped through everyday occurrences to fulfill the Creator's specific purpose He has for each of our lives.

     The definition of an analogy is a comparison in which an idea or a thing is compared to another thing that is quite different from it. It aims at explaining that idea or thing by comparing it to something that is familiar.

The Making of a Woman

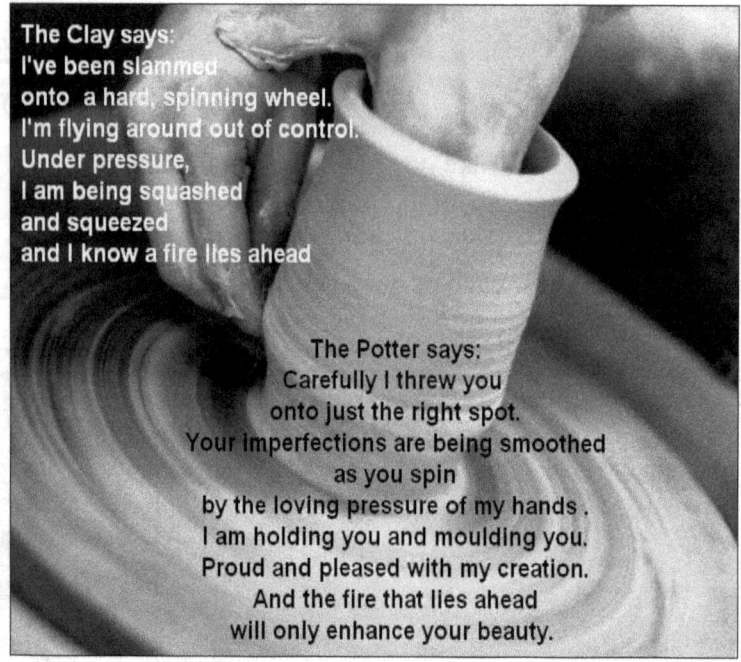

The Clay says:
I've been slammed
onto a hard, spinning wheel.
I'm flying around out of control.
Under pressure,
I am being squashed
and squeezed
and I know a fire lies ahead

The Potter says:
Carefully I threw you
onto just the right spot.
Your imperfections are being smoothed
as you spin
by the loving pressure of my hands .
I am holding you and moulding you.
Proud and pleased with my creation.
And the fire that lies ahead
will only enhance your beauty.

But now, O LORD, thou art our father; we are the clay, and thou our potter; and we all are the work of thy hand. Isa. 64:8

    The analogy of making pottery is an excellent illustration of how God is at work in our daily lives. The pottery analogy reveals how God has a plan, purpose, and process to help us BECOME who we were meant to be and help us to discover our life work through the same process a Potter uses when he is making a masterpiece: pressure, pain, and sometimes pruning (**ouch!**).

    Let's take a few moments to examine the making of a clay vessel. Becoming a woman of purpose and destiny can be painful however it is one of the most rewarding and fulfilling events in your life.

Imagine beautiful finished clay pots, before they were completed they were just a lump of clay, formless, useless, and worthless without any specific purpose ......

"And the LORD God formed man of the dust of the ground, and breathed into his nostrils the breath of life; and man became a living soul." Genesis 2:7,

The potter does not see simply just a lump of clay or dirt at first glance; he sees a beautiful work of art. He envisions something out of that lump of clay or dirt that can be used for a specific purpose. So he makes a plan and puts it into action. First, the clay must be pliable, moist, and centered. If the clay is not centered when pressure is applied the clay will simply tear apart.

Slowly but surely the clay goes around and an around on the potter's wheel. A wonderful work of art comes to life after a specific amount of time of molding, pulling, pressure and cutting the clay. After the potter forms the clay into the unique form or shape he intends it to be, the clay is set out to dry in the sun or put into the fire. When it is hardened, the clay pot will be ready for its INTENDED (specific) purpose!

The Making of a Woman

"Now we have this treasure in clay jars, so that this extraordinary power may be from God and not from us."
2 Corinthians 4:7

"Now in a large house there are not only gold and silver bowls, but also those of wood and earthenware, some for special use, some for ordinary. So if anyone purifies himself from these things, he will be a special instrument, set apart, useful to the Master, prepared for every good work."
2 Timothy 2:20-21

From the Potter's analogy we learn several valuable lessons:

1. The Potter has a Plan, Procedure, and Purpose for the Clay.
2. The Potter's Procedure – The wheel is the tool used to mold and form the clay; the clay must be free from all impurities; the clay must be pliable and it must be centered while the Potter is forming and shaping it into a wonderful work of art! Applying pressure, stretching, pulling, and cutting, the clay for its intended purpose.
3. The Potter has a Plan on how it will happen. He uses water for the pliability to make it moist for the molding.
4. The Potter has a Purpose specific and unique for the clay; the Potter knows the intended use. The Potter is creating a work of art, a masterpiece.
5. The Potter is making a Vessel of Honor.

- The Potter is (God) • The Clay represent (You) •The Plan (How He will do it) pressure, pulling, and stretching • The Procedure is (The Wheel) which represent Everyday living (going around and around) sometimes it feels like you are going around in a circle (remember to pass your test, with responding correctly, to your everyday challenges in life • The Purpose (Why he did it) to empower you to help others.

The Making of a Woman
Principle

- The Maker of the universe has a [3]master plan, to make you a work of art a master piece to serve.

What is pressuring, pulling, or stretching you right now, every day?
_____
_____
_____
_____

What is your perspective concerning the procedure (this could be a person, your health, finances, an addiction, etc.) right now?
_____
_____
_____
_____

Are you able to connect the dots yet?
_____
_____
_____
_____

---

[3] *Ephesians 2:10*

Piece 10

1st CASE STUDY

> "The struggle of life is one of our greatest blessings. It makes us patient, sensitive, and Godlike. It teaches us that although the world is full of suffering, it is also full of the overcoming of it." -Helen Keller

Hellen Keller *(A Vessel of Honor)*
Educator, Journalist
Born in 1880 – 1968

Life Work: Writer, activist, advocate, and recognized champion of the disabled.

    Helen was born with the senses of sight and hearing, however before she turned two years old, she fell ill with a high fever. When the fever broke a few days later, Keller's mother noticed her daughter no longer responded to her when she rang the bell or if she waved her hand in front of her. Helen had lost both her sight and hearing. The cause of her illness they called it acute congestion of the stomach and the brain, still a mystery.

    Helen's world had become cold and dark, she no longer could see nor hear. As a result of her losing her sight and hearing, Helen was very angry, bitter, and rebellious. Helen would throw violent temper tantrums when she did not get her way. She would kick and pull her nurse's hair

The Making of a Woman

demonstrating all kinds of rage. One day she knocked down her baby sister's cradle.

The baby might have been killed had Helen's mother not caught the baby before she fell. After this near tragedy, Helen's parents almost considered institutionalizing her. They were weary but still loved their daughter. Her mother and father sought help for many years. Finally, they were recommended to Alexander Graham Bell, the inventor of the telephone was also a teacher for the deaf. When Helen met Mr. Bell there was in instant connection between them. He understood her, and soon grew very fond of him as he became the *door* through which Helen would pass from death to life, from isolation to friendship, companionship, knowledge, and love.

Helen grew leaps and bounds under the tutelage of Mr. Bell and he suggested to her parents that they should contact the Perkins Institution in Boston to see if they had a teacher who would be willing to work with Helen. One institution responded with the recommendation of Miss Ann Sullivan. Ann Sullivan was an extraordinary teacher with her own set of challenges. Ann's mother died from tuberculosis when she was eight years old and her younger brother Jimmie was only three. Ann was half blind, and her brother had a hip disorder. Her abusive father was an alcoholic and used to beat her. Years later, he later abandoned both Ann and her brother.

After their father left, Ann and her brother were taken and placed in the State Infirmary in Tewksbury, Massachusetts. Ann and Jimmie were placed with people who had various mental disorders and highly infectious diseases. The place was infested with rats, roaches – only a petition separated them from dead corpses.

Three years later her brother Jimmie died. Ann remained there for an additional four years. She could leave when the hospital failed one of its annual inspections. Before the authorities closed the place, she begged the supervisor to send her to Perkins Institution. Ann was ready for a new beginning.

Ann Sullivan arrived at the Keller's home and after observing a *calmer* Helen, accepted the job to help her learn how to communicate. It took Ann a few weeks to break through Helen's rebellion. When Ann stuck her hands out, she grabbed Helen and gave her a huge hug.

Ann used various methods to teach Helen. She gave Helen a doll then spelled d-o-l-l in her hand using sign language. Helen liked the feel of the doll. So Ann used the doll to stop Helen's unacceptable behavior. Helen would pinch and slap Ann, however Ann would slap and pinch her back. She did not feel sorry for Helen and would continue to spell words in Helen's hand. Eventually, Helen was taken away from her mother and father so that she could really work with her. Ann broke the spirit of rebellion and disobedience off Helen. However, Helen still did not make the connections with words and things but Ann continued to persevere. She was determined to help Helen comprehend the connections of the word D-O-L-L and the actual doll. On April 5, 1887, it happened! Helen finally got it. Later on, she would call it her *Soul Awakening*.

The Making of a Woman

Helen made the connection between running water from a pump and the letters W-A-T-E-R. She understood the mystery of associating thoughts and language. The living word awakened her soul and gave it light, hope, joy, and freedom. Helen had been SET FREE.

"Character cannot be developed in ease and quiet. Only through experience of trial and suffering can the soul be strengthened, ambition inspired, and success achieved."
Helen Keller quotes:

Helen Keller's Seemingly Insurmountable Obstacles:

- Triple deficiency
- Independence gone
- Animalistic behavior
- Rage
- Rebellion
- Stubbornness
- Blind
- Deaf
- Dumb
- The Stigma of being disabled

"Although the world is full of suffering, it is also full of the overcoming of it." ~ Helen Keller

Helen Keller's Victorious Victories

- In 1904, Helen Keller changed History – 1st Blind person to graduate Cum Laude from Radcliffe College in Massachusetts. She earned a Bachelor of Arts degree.
- Accomplished Author
- Gifted Communicator
- A staunch Advocate for people with disabilities
- Political Activist and Advocate
- Campaigned for Women's Suffrage, birth control, Workers' Rights, and Socialism.
- Cofounder of the American Civil Liberties Union (ACLU) in 1920.
- Leader – for the American Foundation for the Blind (AFB)
- An Entertainer, won an Oscar for her life story documentary "The Unconquered".
- Music *aficionado* – would listen to the vibrations of the music with her fingers.
- World Traveler, traveled to over 39 countries over her lifetime.
- Met with World Leaders and Dignitaries – Helen Keller met Presidents Herbert Hoover, Franklin D. Roosevelt, Grover Cleveland, & Lyndon B. Johnson, John Kennedy, Dwight Eisenhower. Helen's friends included Author Mark Twain, Actor Charlie Chaplin, and Statesmen Winston Churchill.
- An American educator Helen Keller overcame the adversity of being blind and deaf to become one of the 20th century's leading humanitarians.

The Making of a Woman

What did you discover?
_____
_____
_____
_____
_____
_____

What motivated you?
_____
_____
_____
_____
_____
_____

What can you apply to your life?
_____
_____
_____
_____
_____
_____

Piece 11

2nd CASE STUDY

> "I looked on child rearing not only as a work of love & duty but as a profession that was fully as interesting & challenging as any honorable profession in the world and one that demanded the best that I could bring to it."   -Rose Kennedy

Rose Kennedy *(A Vessel of Honor)*
Educator, Journalist
Born in 1880 - 1995

Life Work: Mother, writer, activist, fundraiser, matriarch of the Kennedy Dynasty.
Rose Elizabeth Fitzgerald was born in Boston, Massachusetts' North End on July 22, 1890, the eldest child of John F. ("Honey Fitz") and Mary Josephine Hannon Fitzgerald. Rose was first introduced to politics as a child. She was five when her father served as a congressman. After graduating from high school at the age of 16, Rose was also accepted into Wellesley College in Massachusetts but instead was sent to Boston's Convent of the Sacred Heart at her family's request. Retelling her life story at the age of 90 in an interview with Doris Kearns Goodwin, Mrs. Kennedy said,

"My greatest regret was not going to Wellesley College. It is something I have felt a little sad about all my life."

The Making of a Woman

However, she eventually grew fond of the convent school and she said the religious training she received there became the foundation for her life. In her teens, Rose became acquainted with Joseph P. Kennedy at Old Orchard Beach in Maine while their families were vacationing together. After several years, a courtship emerged and on October 7, 1914, Joseph and Rose were married in a modest ceremony at the residence of Cardinal O'Connell who officiated. At the time of their marriage, Joseph Kennedy was making $10,000 a year as a businessman. The couple eventually had nine children: Joseph P. Kennedy Jr. b. 1915, John b. 1917, Rosemary b.1918, Kathleen b. 1920, Eunice b. 1921, Patricia b. 1924, Robert b. 1925, Jean b. 1928 and Edward b. 1932. Their children were born in the first eighteen years of their fifty-five year-long marriage. Rose quickly immersed herself in the business of raising her family.

She schooled her children in the history of the American Democratic tradition and went on to nurture the political ambitions of three sons -- John, Robert, and Edward -- vigorously promoting their careers through grass roots campaigning. Mrs. Kennedy stated she felt completely fulfilled as a full-time homemaker. In her 1974 autobiography, *Times to Remember*, she wrote, "I looked on child rearing not only as a work of love and a duty, but as a profession that was fully as interesting and challenging as any honorable profession in the world and one that demanded the best I could bring to it. What greater aspirations and challenges are there for a mother than the hope of raising a great son or daughter?"

Mrs. Kennedy's Overwhelming Obstacles

- Rose's third child, Rosemary had been born mentally handicapped. She was later institutionalized
- Husband a womanizer
- In 1943 Joe Jr., first son died overseas when his plane exploded on a secret mission
- In 1948, fourth child Kathleen, was killed in a plane crash in Europe
- In 1961, Joe Kennedy, Sr. suffered a severe, debilitating stroke
- On November 22, 1963, John Fitzgerald Kennedy was shot to death in Dallas
- On June 5, 1968, her third son, Robert, was assassinated
- On July 18, 1969, Ted Kennedy was in a major accident killing passenger Mary Jo Kopechne
- Joe Kennedy died in 1968

The Making of a Woman

Rose Kennedy found solace in religion and her restraint was strengthened by her faith in God as she faced the public time and time again with poise and dignity. Mrs. Kennedy once said in her 1974 autobiography,

"There have been times when I felt I was one of the most fortunate people in the world, almost as if Providence, or Fate, or Destiny, as you like, had chosen me for special favors."

Mrs. Kennedy was considered by many to be a model parent. *"Children,"* she said, *"should be stimulated by their parents to see, touch, know, understand and appreciate."*

Mrs. Kennedy's Outstanding Victories

- Husband became a multimillionaire
- John F. Kennedy - United States Representative (1947–1953) United States Senator (1953–1960) **President of the United States** (1961–1963
- Robert F. Kennedy - United States Attorney General (1961–1964)
   United States Senator (1965–1968)
- Jean A. Kennedy – United States Attorney General (1961 – 1964)
- Edward T. Kennedy- United States Senator (1962–2009)
- Patricia H. Kennedy - Journalist and film production assistant
- Eunice M. Kennedy - International Advocate for the developmentally disabled. Founded the Special Olympics International
- Joseph F. Kennedy Jr. - United States Navy Aviator
- In 1951, Pope Pius XII granted Kennedy the title of *Countess* in recognition of her exemplary motherhood and many charitable works

The Making of a Woman

What did you discover?
_____
_____
_____
_____
_____
_____

What motivated you?
_____
_____
_____
_____
_____
_____

What can you apply to your life?
_____
_____
_____
_____
_____
_____

Piece 12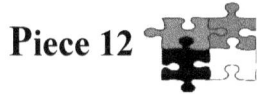

3rd CASE STUDY

> I am a woman who came from the cotton fields of the South. From there I was promoted to the washtub. From there I was promoted to the cook kitchen. And from there I promoted myself into the business of manufacturing hair goods and preparations....I have built my own factory on my own ground.   - Madam C.J. Walker

Sarah Breedlove *(A Vessel of Honor)*
Entrepreneur & Philanthropist
Born in 1867 – 1919

Life Work: Pioneer of Black Hair Care Industry in America and beyond.

Madame C.J. Walker was born Sarah Breedlove on December 23, 1867, on a cotton plantation near Delta, Louisiana. Her parents, Owen and Minerva were recently freed slaves. Sarah was their fifth child and was the first in her family to be free-born. Her mother, Minerva Breedlove died in 1874 and her father, Owen passed away the following year, both due to unknown causes. Sarah became an orphan at the age of seven. After her parents' passing, Sarah was sent to live with

The Making of a Woman

her sister, Louvinia and her brother in law. The three moved to Vicksburg, Mississippi in 1877, where Sarah picked cotton and did household work although no documentation exists verifying her employment at the time.

At age fourteen to escape both her oppressive work environment and the frequent mistreatment she endured at the hands of her brother-in-law, Sarah married a man named Moses McWilliams. On June 6, 1885, Sarah gave birth to a daughter, A'Lelia. When Moses died two years later, Sarah and A'Lelia moved to St. Louis where Sarah's brothers had established themselves as barbers. Sarah found work as a washerwoman earning $1.50 a day—enough to send her daughter to the city's public school. Sarah also attended public night school whenever she could.

While in St. Louis, Breedlove met her second husband Charles J. Walker who worked in advertising. During this time, Sarah began to experience hair thinning like so many other African Americans during the mid-1800s. Sarah was ambitious and she developed her own hair product – almost unheard of for that time period. Sarah, changed her name to Mrs. C.J. Walker and began to go door-to-door across the United States selling her products. Soon, she became the first African American woman to become a self- made millionaire. Against all odds and during a time when women were manual laborers and earned $1.50 a day. Madame C.J. Walker became a millionaire!

Madame Walker's Obstacles to Overcome

- Born to slaves
- Very poor, picked cotton for a living, wages $1.50 a day
- No formal education
- Orphaned at the age of seven
- Mistreated and oppressed
- Married at the age of fourteen to escape harsh treatment from family member
- Daughter born and husband died two years later
- Married three times, divorced twice
- Societal conditions – Lynching and other gross mistreatment of blacks was the norm
- Majority of black women were sharecroppers, washer women, or housekeepers

Madame C. J Walker's Triumphant Victories

- Pioneered the hair care industry 100 years later, now a multi-billion-dollar industry
- Launched her own product line
- Became the first self-made black woman millionaire
- Founder of Walker Beauty School
- Empowered over 25,000 black women worldwide
- International businesswoman
- Pioneered direct sells
- Recognized at the National Business Hall of Fame at the Museum of Science Industry in Chicago, Illinois
- Recognized in National of Women Hall of Fame in New York, New York
- Traveled across the United States, Central of America and the Caribbean

The Making of a Woman

- Motivated her agents to give back to their own community
- Madame C.J Walkers' work still lives on through the Madame Walker Theater in Indianapolis, Indiana.

What did you discover?
_____
_____
_____
_____
_____

What motivated you?
_____
_____
_____
_____
_____

What can you apply to your life?
_____
_____
_____
_____
_____

Piece 13

The Making of a Woman
Body, Soul & Spirit

Health is very important to us fulfilling our life assignment.

As discussed in an earlier chapter, the body is the physical part of you that everyone sees, it houses the soul and spirit. The composition of the human body is made up of a number of certain elements including carbon, calcium, and phosphorus. The study of the human body includes anatomy and physiology. The body is a very important subject matter because it carries the real you all the way around. You must take care of it by staying fit and healthy.

$^{26\text{-}27}$ I don't know about you, but I'm running hard for the finish line. I'm giving it everything I've got. No sloppy living for me! I'm staying alert and in top condition. I'm not going to get caught napping, telling everyone else all about it and then missing out myself (1 Cor 9:26-27 Message Bible)

~ Being victorious is to know what each part of you needs
Lisa A. Brown~

The Making of a Woman

Testimony 1

Feeling young and being healthy is everything
Tao Porchon - Lynch

Body

[4]Tao Porchon – Lynch is a 96-year-old yoga master, actress, model, dancer, and activist who had to overcome many obstacles in her long and active life. From the very start, she never knew her mother as she died giving birth. Years later, the death of her husband after twenty years of marriage and most recent, a hip replacement at the age of 93. All these obstacles would have taken a toll on the average nonagenarian but despite her trials, she is still up every morning at 5 o'clock in the morning teaching yoga. A primary function of yoga includes meditation. Ms. Porchon- Lynch believes meditation is a key component to her healthy state of being. Some of Porchon- Lynch's accomplishments were cited in the May 2012 edition of Guinness World Records as she was recognized as the world's oldest yoga instructor at age 93 years old. She has been featured on mainstream media with several appearances on the **NBC Today Morning Show**, **CNN**, and **The Steve Harvey Show**. She is an award-winning world class dancer. She marched with Mahatma Gandhi and participated in demonstrations with Former French Leader, General Charles de Gaulle and Martin Luther King Jr.

There is nothing you cannot do
Tao Porchon – Lynch

---

[4] http://www.taoporchon-lynch.com/

Physical fitness

10 leading causes of deaths in [5]American women according to Center of Disease for Women.

All Females, All Ages	Percent*
1) Heart disease	22.9
2) Cancer	21.8
3) Stroke	6.1
4) Chronic lower respiratory diseases	6.0
5) Alzheimer's disease	4.7
6) Unintentional injuries	3.7
7) Diabetes	2.8
8) Influenza and pneumonia	2.3
9) Kidney disease	1.8
10) Septicemia	1.5

Maintaining a healthy balanced lifestyle is the key to good health along with prayer. According to medical reports the four major causes of deaths are contributed to lifestyle, smoking, lack of physical exercise, drinking, and eating the wrong foods.

5

http://www.cdc.gov/dhdsp/data_statistics/fact_sheets/fs_women_heart.htm

The Making of a Woman

The Caloric Balance Equation When it comes to maintaining healthy weight for a lifetime, the bottom line is – **calories do count!** Weight management is all about balance—balancing the number of calories you consume with the number of calories your body uses or "burns off".

- A *calorie* is defined as a unit of energy supplied by food. A calorie is a calorie regardless of its source. Whether you're eating carbohydrates, fats, sugars, or proteins, all of them contain calories.
- *Caloric balance* is like a scale. To remain in balance and maintain your body weight, the calories consumed (from foods) must be balanced by the calories used (in normal body functions, daily activities, and exercise).

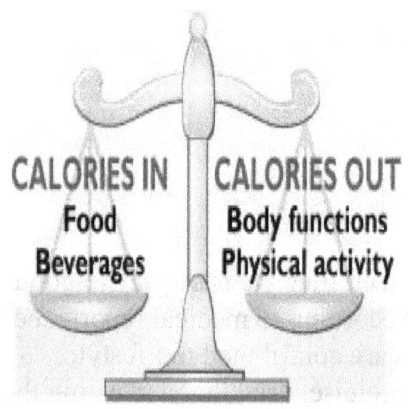

CALORIES IN
Food
Beverages

CALORIES OUT
Body functions
Physical activity

If you are maintaining your current body weight, you are in caloric balance. If you need to gain weight or to lose weight, you'll need to tip the balance scale in one direction or another to achieve your goal. If you need to tip the balance scale in the direction of losing weight, keep in mind that it takes approximately 3,500 calories below your calorie needs to lose a pound of body fat. To lose about 1 to 2 pounds per week, you'll need to reduce your caloric intake by 500 - 1000 calories per day.

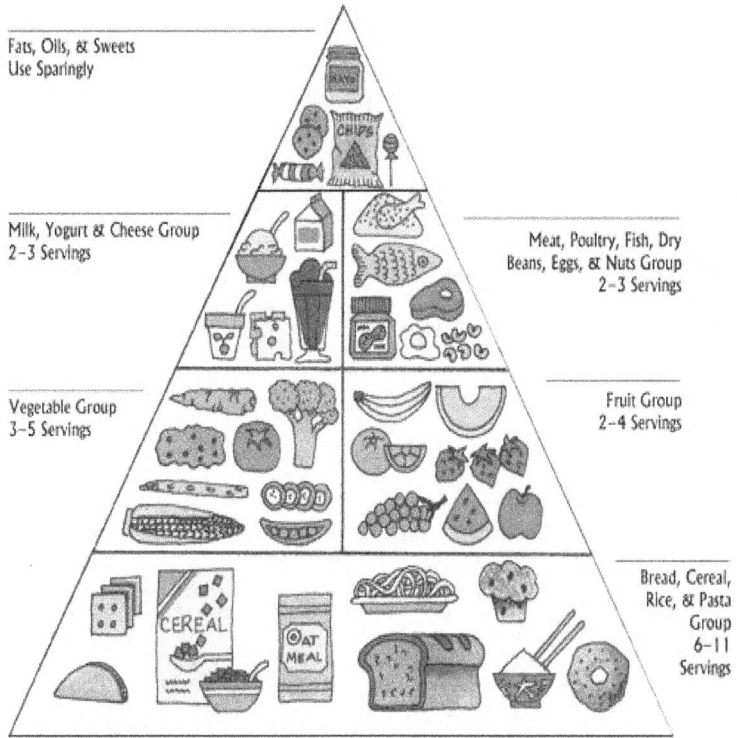

  To learn how many calories, you are currently eating, begin writing down the foods you eat and the beverages you drink each day. By writing down what you eat and drink, you will become more aware of caloric intake. Also, begin writing down the physical activity you do each day and the length of time you do it. Here are simple tools to assist you:

The Making of a Woman

Physical activities (both daily activities and exercise) help to tip the balance scale by increasing the calories you expend each day.

Recommended Physical Activity Levels

- **Set a goal to exercise.** For example: 2 hours and 30 minutes (150 minutes) of moderate-intensity aerobic activity (i.e., brisk walking) every week and muscle-strengthening activities on 2 or more days a week that work all major muscle groups (legs, hips, back, abdomen, chest, shoulders, and arms).
- **Increasing the intensity of physical activity** or the amount of time that you are physically active can have even greater health benefits and may be needed to control body weight according to the Centers for Disease Control Women's Health Division.
- **Commit to a physical lifestyle:** The single most important thing people can do to prevent the buildup of belly fat and get rid of existing belly fat is commit to physical activity, and better yet, a physical lifestyle.
- **Move around, fidget:** Here's something else most people don't know. Fidgeting is good for you. It's considered a non-exercise physical activity and it's an important way to burn energy. You get more health benefits if in addition to exercising, you are a more fidgety, more active person the rest of the day. This means gesturing while you're talking, tapping your foot, just simply moving around.
- **And try not to sit too much:** Studies have shown that people who sit eight to nine hours a day, even if they exercise the recommended 150 minutes per week, do not

get the same benefits of exercising as people who are more active throughout the day.

If you have to sit most of the day for your job, try to find some ways to move:

- Take small breaks throughout the day to walk around
- Use your lunch hour to take a walk
- Take the stairs instead of the elevator, if possible
- Do stretching exercises at your desk
- Just do your best to move around as much as you can

- **Redefine 'rest':** Have an active hobby and if you don't already have one, develop one. It is very important to engage in some kind of sport or activity whether it's a group activity or something you can do alone. Essentially if an activity is pleasant to you, you'll continue to do it according to Rush University Medical Center, Chicago, Illinois.

Remember, moderate-intensity physical activity is that "magic pill" a lot of people are looking for because the health benefits go far beyond keeping your waistline trim. Not only can it reduce your risk of cancer, stroke, diabetes, and heart attacks, but studies have shown that physical activity can significantly improve the moods of patients with major depressive disorders.

Now let's plan for fitness!

The Making of a Woman

Answer the following question:

What are your current:
Body Goals?

_____

_____

_____

_____

_____

_____

_____

_____

_____

Piece 14

The Making of a Woman
Body, Soul & Spirit

Put your ear down close to your soul and listen hard
Ann Sexton

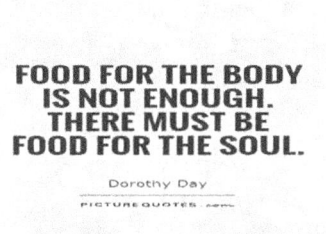

FOOD FOR THE BODY IS NOT ENOUGH. THERE MUST BE FOOD FOR THE SOUL.
Dorothy Day

Just as important as the body or physical part in the previous section stated, the soul is also a very important part of our being. The soul houses our mind, will, and emotions. It is the part of us where negative or positive deposits have been made. This is where soul ties are formed, and the unhealthy ones must be broken. A healthy soul must be nourished and taken care of.

Physical activities like painting, bicycling, and meditating, is food for the soul.

Put yourself in order

The Making of a Woman

Testimony 2

Soul

Self-Development

Lisa Nicholas is a motivational coach, author and speaker. During her many speaking engagements Lisa openly shares with others how she has transformed her life. Lisa was on welfare nineteen years ago overcoming issues such as, low self-esteem, battles with weight, and her overall appearance. Lisa comes from a real but all too common place of life struggles and obstacles: being poor: not being able to buy diapers for her son and not being able to withdraw $1 from the Automatic Teller Machine (ATM). Lisa's hardships captivate all who hear her stories as she tells of harsh winters when she had to wrap her son up with fabric to keep him warm while the father was away in prison. Tired and feed-up with the *low life*, one day Lisa declared and decreed to her son "I will never be this broke or broken again in my life!" Lisa made up her mind that she would begin to recreate herself, mind, body and soul. She began to attend conferences and workshops – anywhere she could receive and retain positive information. Today, Lisa often jokes about the time she attended a particular conference over and over again in order to get the concept. She responded, "I am thorough learner not a fast one." Today, Lisa is a millionaire and a best-selling author of six books. Lisa has been featured on major television outlets including **CNN**, the **Steve Harvey Show** and **Oprah** and she serves as the CEO of *Motivating the Masses*. Lisa and her many endeavors have a global presence reaching and serving millions of people.

How the soul is designed to work

Remember our look at the 3 parts of the soul: mind, will, and emotions? Now we're going to examine the template or the prototype by which God designed us so that we can use it as a standard to evaluate how our souls are *actually* functioning.

Using the diagram below, this is how this triune (3-part) nature of man is to operate.

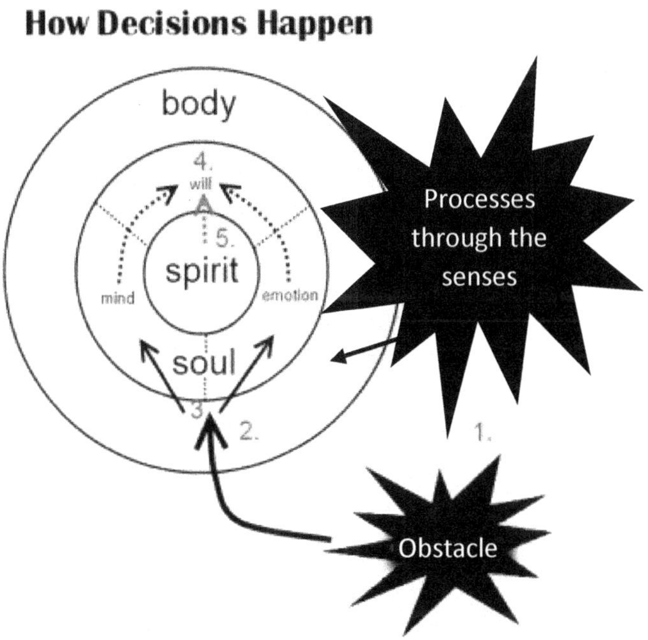

How Decisions Happen

[Diagram: concentric circles labeled body (outer), soul containing mind, will, emotion, and spirit (inner, labeled 5). Numbers 1-4 indicate sequence. Arrows point from "Obstacle" to the soul, then "Processes through the senses" leading into the body/soul.]

First, some (information, challenge, obstacle) +thought or idea triggers an emotion.

Second, you received the information (Challenge or Obstacle) from an internal source (thought or idea) or an external source e.g. you heard, or witnessed (sight) an event.

The Making of a Woman

Third, the information is relayed to the mind and emotions (the soul). The mind's job is to evaluate the information based on sensory factors (what you see or hear or feel). The emotions combine with any physical responses from the body.

Fourth. Next, the mind and emotions pass on their "conclusions" about the situation to the will.

Fifth. Finally, a person's spirit engages with their will. The will draws insight from several sources: (a) the Word of God, (b) Counsel of fellow-believers, and (c) the Spirit of God. All these factors are included in the process of making right decisions or choices in your life. These steps must be repeated over and over again to condition the "Soul". It's like a work-out for the soul!

If you have not given your life to Jesus Christ, then you will process information or challenges from other sources friends, family or others, Dr. Phil and so on and you may not get the results you desire. There is much on this subject-matter, I encourage you to gain more insight on how the soul work, it will prove to be priceless, in your life.

Repeat this affirmation several times or (300) times before you go to sleep for 30 days:

Forgiveness is good for my soul, letting go is a must for my soul.

. . . and if you still feel bound . . . then confess, I am loosed from all physical, mental, or emotional soul ties in Jesus name, Amen. (Adapted from Philippian 2:9)

Another great affirmation:

I forgive and release all wounds intentional and unintentional from my soul.

The Making of a Woman

What are your current: Soul/Goals?

_____

_____

_____

_____

_____

_____

_____

_____

_____

_____

Piece 15

The Making of a Woman
Body, Soul & **Spirit**

Now let's take a look back to better understand where we are now. First, we looked at the "Body" and how it is the outward part of our person. We examined how we must take care of our bodies with balanced nutrition and intense physical activity. Next, we looked at the "Soul" and all the 3 parts that make the soul the central warehouse of our mind, will and emotions. We concluded that our soul must be trained and conditioned to make the right choices and decisions, which leads us to our next topic: The spirit.

The spirit is the most important part of us, "We are a spirit and we possess a soul, and we live in a body."

(1 Thessalonians 5:23)

The spirit which is also referred to as the *inner man*, the *human spirit*, *true self* and the *higher self*.

What does this mean? First you must discover and acknowledge your "spirit", a powerful place inside you.

"In this place is hidden your treasure and your true potential". (2 Corinthians 4:7)

The Making of a Woman

All the women featured in this book have tapped into their true power and have found the strength to overcome life obstacles. How did they do this? They focused on their spirit that is, the power within. **<u>Simply put, the spirit should be the center your life</u>**. **<u>If your life is centered on your spirit you will become unstoppable</u>**.

What is a center? It is how you perceive the world around you or how you build your life.

Let's look at a few common centers. As women we tend to make spouses, family, money, work, possessions pleasure, principles, church or friends the focus of our existence. Each one of these centers will cause you to respond differently. **However, when you make your spirit your center, you will live from the inside out. You will be able to overcome any outside distractions or obstacles**, why? Your peace is from the inside out and not from the outside. Let's look at a woman who lives from the inside out.

Testimony 3

Spirit

Joyce Myer – Christian Author and speaker.

Joyce Myers (born Pauline Joyce Hutchison) serves as a great spiritual role model. Affectionately known as "Joyce".

Joyce has been on a campaign of "openness" about many of her life struggles and obstacles. Unashamed, Joyce shared for many years she had suffered from sexual abuse from her father. This horrible experience left her controlling, manipulative, and rebellious – Joyce contends this is why her first marriage lasted just five years. However, when she found the Lord and received the Holy Spirit, studied the Word of God and later was called into the ministry – everything suddenly changed – eventually for the good. At first, she was rejected by her peers and faced financial challenges. According to Joyce, she always had more bills left than money. She had to believe God for the additional money every month.

A life of constant tragedy, her brother was found dead in an abandoned building left for many days. Sadly, Joyce had to identify his badly decomposed body. In light of this tragedy, her mother had a nervous breakdown.

The Making of a Woman

Good News! In spite of all her heart aches, pains and struggles, Joyce Meyer is now a world-renowned preacher, and author of several books that have sold in the millions. She produces several TV programs that air to over two-thirds of the world.

Here's the best part, after just a few years in ministry and as she evolved and began healing from her life traumas, Joyce met and later married Dave Meyers. They have been married for over forty years!

Joyce continues to be faithful and now helps hurting and abused people all over the world. She is financially secure, and a powerful, spiritual leader.

What are your current:
spiritual/ Goals

_____

_____

_____

_____

_____

_____

_____

_____

_____

Piece 16

Role - Modeling

All three areas Body, Soul and Spirit equal a Vessel of Honor.

*R*uth is a remarkable Vessel of Honor and serves as another great role model. First let's look at the obstacles this Biblical woman of God had to overcome.

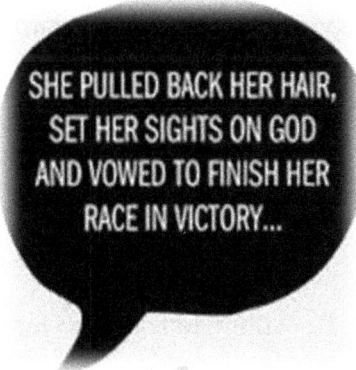
SHE PULLED BACK HER HAIR, SET HER SIGHTS ON GOD AND VOWED TO FINISH HER RACE IN VICTORY...

Typically, in ancient times when a husband dies, the young widow was to stay with another male relative to provide and care for her. In Ruth's case all the male relatives had died therefore she was poor and very much alone according to the laws and customs. All these significant losses could have made Ruth bitter and confused in the natural realm. Fortunately, Ruth had one relative she could reach out to – her mother in-law Naomi. Naomi was a strong and committed woman of God.

Ruth admired and believed in Naomi to boldly declare in obedience, "Where you go, I will go, and your God shall be my God." Ruth trusted Naomi and must have sensed a real connection to her destiny to leave everything

The Making of a Woman

that was familiar to her; her home town, family and friends and follow Naomi to a strange and different land. After arriving in the new land, Ruth worked relentlessly in the fields and one day, Ruth's faithfulness paid off. Ruth received a huge bonus for her obedience. She was recognized by Boaz, a wealthy man known throughout the land. Boaz fell in love with Ruth and they married and later had a child, Jesse who would later become the grandfather of King David, a relative of Jesus Christ.

Ruth found supernatural favor and was recognized in the Proverb 31 Hall of Fame as a" Virtuous Woman".

Lessons from Ruth life story:

- Be willing to leave the familiar your place of comfort (**ouch!***).*
- Ruth was willing to stay connected to her destiny (her life work).
- Ruth had a discerning heart that was resolved to stay and be obedient.
- Be willing to be mentored – She listen to Naomi's advice.
- Be a hard worker. Ruth went to work daily.
- Be courageous

Principle:

- Sowing and Reaping (What I sow is what I reap).

I tore myself away from the safe comfort, or certainties through my love for truth – and truth rewarded me.
Simone de BeauVoir

Piece 17

Vision

Without a vision my people perish ~ Proverbs 29:13

What is a vision? A vision or vision statement should reflect your values and what you believe.

Take a moment to write down your vision statement below. Your vision statement should be in the present tense (the now) and the statement should be less than 50 to 60 words.

Example #1. I am a woman of God. I am blessed and highly favored of the Lord. I prosper in every godly endeavor. My life belongs to the Lord and I live to please and honor Him. God is my only source. He provides for me each and every day and I am blessed to be a blessing to others.

Example #2. I am healthy. I weigh my ideal weight (150). I eat only good food. I will double my income next year by this time. I have my high school diploma, (GED, Associate, or Bachelor's degree)… I am married to a loving and a giving man and so forth. . ."

My Vision Statement:
_____
_____
_____
_____

The Making of a Woman

God has a purpose or vision for our lives before we were born. Jeremiah 29:11

And the LORD answered me, and said, "Write the vision, and make it plain upon tables, that he may run that reads it".

Habakkuk 2:2

It's never too late to get a vision. Many trials and tribulations may have come into your life but I decree and declare today, a **TURNAROUND**! Regardless of the calamity, complacency, or devastation, God will never allow anything to come upon you without a vision or a P-L-A-N to get a greater glory!

See your vision through the eyes of faith. See yourself turning your obstacles into opportunities.

"A vision is a mental picture of a future state"
Casey Treat

Now that you have your vision statement, think on your vision day and night. By doing this, your vision will go deep down inside of you and before you know it – your vision will manifest from the inside of you into reality.

Repeat 10 times:

I can achieve my vision and I will overcome each and every obstacle that comes my way!

Piece 18

40-Day Power Pack Plan

*The Making of a Woman
Overcoming every Obstacle & Obtaining Victory*

Read, Believe • Speak it
• Think it • See it

Suggested Reading:

Mark 9:23
Proverbs 18:21

Philippians 4:13

Proverbs 23:7
Genesis 13:15

Deuteronomy 30:1
Joshua 1:8

The Making of a Woman

Believe • Speak these affirmations •Think on • Write them • Repeat them each day

1. I am beautiful
2. I am powerful
3. My soul is free, mind, body and spirit
4. I have favor everywhere I go especially at my place of employment
5. I am lovely, I am loved, I am forgiving, I am caring, I am changing
6. I am living my life on purpose, I am living out my purpose
7. I am enjoying my life everyday
8. I am in the now, I let go of the past
9. I am optimisitc
10. I am free
11. I am healed
12. I am at peace even under pressure
13. I decree and declare that I am priceless, powerful, and prosperous
14. I let go of my past and I embrace my present and new process of change
15. I say yes to my intended purpose
16. I affirm that all things are working for my good
17. I affirm that my body is working at its optimum level
18. I affirm I go above and beyond the call of duty
19. I can do all things through Christ that strengthens me

20. I call into being a persistent presence of a support network for my life
21. I decree and declare I will overcome every obstacle that comes my way
22. I declare and decree that I have positive expectations and the tendency to frame events in a constructive light
23. I affirm a sense of spiritual involvement
24. I confess I can adapt to changing situations
25. I confess that when I am overwhelmed, I immediately go into prayer and meditation, along with deep breathing
26. I affirm and confess I crave for daily physical activity
27. I commit to identifying and communicating my feelings
28. I decree and declare I am thankful and I have an attitude of gratitude
29. I confess I create a positive environment for myself
30. I am Prosperous
31. I am a Giver
32. I am a woman of character
33. I am a woman who chooses to eat healthy
34. I am a woman who chooses to disassociate with anything or anybody that does not mean me well
35. I am a woman who chooses to stay physically fit
36. I am a woman who chooses to live a debt free life style
37. I am free from stress
38. I never second guess the leading of my spirit also known as a "gut feeling"
39. I do it now, I will not procrastinate
40. I trust the Potter of my soul, and His plan, and purpose for my life

The Making of a Woman

40 Days of monitoring your accomplishments

Journal what you are working on?
E.g. becoming more healthy or wealthy…

[Month]

Sund	Mon	Tues	Wed	Thurs	Frida	Satur
drink 8 cups/waters meditate volunteer	1	2	3	4	5	6
7	8	9	10	11	12	13
14	15	16	17	18	19	20
21	22	23	24	25	26	27
28	29	30	31	32	33	34
35	36	37	38	39	40	

Piece 19

Bonus

What do you see?

In my conclusion, I want to end with several experiences to deepen your insight and to challenge you to look at things different.

What do you see?

Do you see a young lady looking away or an old lady looking down?

Depending on how you look at it will determine what you see. What is the young woman's ear; might be the old woman's eye. What is the young woman's necklace; might be the old woman's mouth. The picture hasn't really changed. You just emphasize different parts of it and assign them different meaning.

The Making of a Woman

Look at these two arrows. Which horizontal line is the longest?

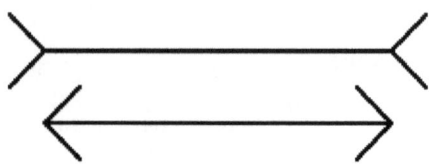

They are the same size.

.

Are those letters? Or are they just lines and blotches on the paper? What do you see?

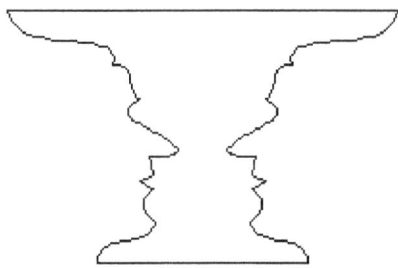

Do you see a vase or do you see two faces looking at each other?

The meaning of something will change when you look at it differently. You can look at anything deeply and it will have a different meaning. Every obstacle can be overcome with the right perspective.

~ What you see is your reality ~

You were created to be a Vessel of Honor, power, strength, value, courage, integrity, wealth, longevity, and excellence, can you see now?

Now shine in the midst of a dark world.

The Making of a Woman

(The Natural Perspective) *I wanted a perfect ending. Now I've learned, the hard way, that some poems don't rhyme, and some stories don't have a clear beginning, middle, and end. Life is about not knowing, having to change, taking the moment and making the best of it, without knowing what's going to happen next. Delicious Ambiguity."*
Gilda Radner

(The Spiritual Perspective) *I trust the Sovereignty of God, and to know that He has a plan for His creation. He uses everyday occurrences to bring me closer to my intended purpose (life work). However, I cannot succumb to the misfortunes, calamities, and devastations, and other unexplainable mishaps, mentally, emotionally, physically, socially or economically that may happen in my life. I must know that the dots will eventually connect. No part is the whole, and everything that happens in my life will lead me into my INTENDED PURPOSE (SERVICE). God is the Potter (Master Craftsman), and I, are the clay (A Work of Art Gods Masterpiece).*

Piece 20

My story

Hello and Blessings! I pray I have empowered, encouraged, and educated you so that you can live strong in your life work. I am 49 years old, and single at the present moment. However, I have great expectations that God will send the right one for me… not Mr. Right but the one He has for me.

I have overcome many obstacles just to share a few: I had to overcome looking for love in all the wrong places. At sixteen, I gave the most precious part of me away to someone I really didn't know. This opened up the door to countless broken relationships trying to fill a void I was completely oblivious I had. This led to a lifestyle of alcohol which I previously vowed I would *never* drink; for it was alcohol that destroyed my mother at the age of thirty-seven and before that her mother who died when she was only two years old.

My mother was separated from her siblings and placed in a foster home where she later met my father. She married him when she was sixteen years old, and needless to say, the marriage ended in divorce. The separation from her brothers and sisters early in life also caused my mother a lot of hurt and unfortunately, she turned to alcohol to ease the pain. Divorced and struggling with two children to raise, my mom continued her downward spiral looking for love and a year later she had my little sister. Now with three mouths to feed, my mother met JL who claimed my little sister as his daughter. JL was a hardworking man that believed in paying

The Making of a Woman

his bills and that children should be respectful. Even though my mother was an alcoholic she taught us many things including respect for elders and how to survive. My brother, sister and I constantly stayed on her mind, she never forgot about her three babies. I remember one time when my mother decided to leave my stepfather and get her own place in *K Town* on the west side of Chicago. My mother had to exterminate the house to get rid of the roaches before we could move in. Little did she know that made the problem worse, the whole house was covered in roaches, the walls were brown and they were falling off the ceiling!

My stepfather would come by and check up on us even though he and my mother were no longer together. He would give her money to buy food and give her pocket money to buy her cigarettes. For a treat, she'd get herself *Canadian Midst* and beer. JL was a good man but he had a couple of problems: he was a womanizer and he would fight my mother.

Looking back, when my mom was with my stepfather we always had food. One day I opened up the refrigerator to fix dinner for my brother and sister only to discover there was only one head of lettuce, and in the pantry, was a can of tomato soup. I took the head of lettuce, rinsed it off, cut it up, and opened the can of tomato soup added some water. I think we had some pepper and I made my sister and brother a pretty decent dinner. Times were indeed tough . . .

Through it all, my mother seemed to deal with her low self-esteem and depression. There was never a time my mother did not have a man. It was like having a *piece of man* made her feel like a woman. However, the men she typically ended up with were fighters. My mother met another man named Mr. Will. One summer, Mr. Will took all of us down south to visit relatives. I remember it was so hot AND there were *big* mosquitos! I recall so many memories: going out to pump water for *Big Momma*. Big Momma was Mr. Will's mother.

Big Momma could cook! I especially loved how she would prepare a delicious breakfast: homemade grits, scrambled eggs, toast, bacon, country sausages, and biscuits. Every meal we had a choice of milk or juice. Wow! I remember thinking to myself, *this is great*! But the biggest drawback to those visits -- the mosquitos! I have the scars from those bites to this day. Another big deal for me was the wooden outhouse. I had never seen an outhouse before! I could not imagine having to go outside every day to use the bathroom. . . Just as I can recall the sweet beautiful memories of going south, I also remember the bitter times as well. My mom, Will and a small group of locals had been drinking.

Not usually a problem but my mother had a bad habit of talking a lot and when she drank – the talking got worse. One day I remember her and Will got into it. The fight turned ugly when he took the heel of his heavy cowboy boot and rammed it into my mother's right eye. Blood was running down her face, her eye was swollen, and all the skin was gone. The wound was so bad you could see the flesh and the bone. Right then and there, she decided Will was not the guy for her. Unfortunately, my mother didn't have a lot of money but she told me, "Mommy has to go but I will be back to get you and your brother" and she left. I was a little

The Making of a Woman

scared at first but Big Momma took care of us and we were blessed to have her in our lives. One day after my mother left, I got an ear infection. Big Momma said, "I will take care of you." She brought me close to her and poured some peroxide down in my ear and whatever was in my ear bubbled right up and out. From that point on, I felt safe even though for the first time in my life my mother was not around. Months passed and it seemed like years, and one day, my mother came back to get us.

At the end of her life, I realized my mother never tapped into her spirit to unleash her true potential. She gave up hope and died. I believe she was looking for love in all the wrong places and ultimately died from a broken heart. All this pain caused her to drink her life away and eventually die from psoriasis of the liver.

As a result of all the pain, I had seen, I to enter into abusive relationships. In my marriage, I did have to overcome manipulation, domination, and controlling spirits along with other psychological abuse. When I accepted Jesus Christ as my personal Lord and Savior, I found the love I had been looking for all my life and today I am a fulfilled single saved mother raising three beautiful girls from a marriage that lasted sixteen years. I own my own business. I am the pastor of a growing congregation, and I am the founder of RCEDC (Rainbow Covenant Economic Development Center), an organization that facilitates jobs, and brings educational development, and spiritual empowerment to individuals, and households in the community. All my obstacles are now viewed as opportunities for God to get the Glory out of my life.

The love that I was looking for, I now give it away. PRAISE OUR CREATOR!

To use the earlier illustration, *the Potter used all bad things to shape and form me to His intended purpose.* The Potter had a plan to free me from my past and every relationship that did not serve His purpose. Just like the clay the Potter uses, God had to remove all of the impurities. I had to learn how to let go and forgive others and myself. My life has become more and more centered on the Potter's wheel. I am now in my intended purpose, my life work. All the pieces came together once I said *yes* to the Maker of my body, soul and spirit.

Since I have been obedient and walking with the Lord, life has become sweeter and sweeter because I trust the Lord and I believe He knows what is best for me. My job is to maintain a victorious attitude and the right perspective. He is the Capable Creator of the Universe!

I can't end this book without extending the invitation to make Jesus Christ your Lord and Savior. In this place or state of being is where a New Life really begins.

You have made many decisions; however, this is the BEST decision you can ever make.

I'm not talking about joining a church or finding religion. Would you pray with me today? Just say, "Lord Jesus, I repent of my sins. I ask you to come into my heart. I make you Lord and Savior of my Life."

Sister, if you 've prayed that prayer, I believe you have been "born again." I encourage you to attend a good, Bible-based church and keep God first in your life.

The Making of a Woman

I love you, I will be praying for you. I am believing for Gods intended purpose to be fulfilled in your life. For more information on how you can grow stronger in your spiritual life or how to discover your intended purpose in life, please feel free to contact me. I would love to hear from you:

Please write or call:
(O) 773.417.2942
Email: LBRCEDC@Gmail.com or visited
Website: www.LBhelpingothers.com

Lisa A. Brown
5816 W. Chicago Ave
Chicago, IL 60651

Scripture Meditation for new perspective

"For I know the plans I have for you," declares the LORD, "plans to prosper you and not to harm you, plans to give you hope and a future" Jeremiah 29:11 (NIV)

But we have this treasure in earthen vessels, that the excellency of the power may be of God, and not of us.[8] We are troubled on every side, yet not distressed; we are perplexed, but not in despair; [9] Persecuted, but not forsaken; cast down, but not destroyed; 2 Corinthians 4:7 -9 (KJV)

God created man like him, to take dominion
Then God said, "Let us make a man[i]—someone like ourselves, * to be the master of all life upon the earth and in the skies and in the seas." 27 So God made man like his Maker. (TLB Gen 1:26, 27)

God formed man from dust:
And the LORD God formed man of the dust of the ground, and breathed into his nostrils the breath of life; and man became a living soul." Gen 2:7 (KJV)

God owns everything and everybody
"The earth is the LORD's, and everything in it, the world, and all who live in it;" Psalm 24:1(MSG)

God is capable and intelligent:
"Oh yes, you shaped me first inside, then out; you formed me in my mother's womb. I thank you, High God—you're breathtaking! Body and soul, I am marvelously made! I worship in adoration—what a creation! You know me inside and out; you know every bone in my body; you know exactly how I was

The Making of a Woman

made, bit by bit, how I was sculpted from nothing into something. Like an open book, you watched me grow from conception to birth; all the stages of my life were spread out before you, the days of my life all prepared before I'd even lived one day."   139:13-16 (MSG).

God's creation doubts him:
> 16 [Oh, your perversity!] You turn things upside down! Shall the potter be considered of no more account than the clay? Shall the thing that is made say of its maker, He did not make me; or the thing that is formed say of him who formed it, He has no understanding? Isaiah29:16 (AMP)

God's Creatures our striving against their maker in society:
> 9 Woe to him who strives with his

Maker! —a worthless piece of broken pottery among other pieces equally worthless [and yet presuming to strive with his Maker]! Shall the clay say to him who fashions it, what do you think you are making? Or, your work has no handles? Isaiah 45:9 (AMP)

God is our Maker:
> 8 "But now, O LORD, thou art our father; we are the clay, and thou our potter; and we all are the work of thy hand." Isaiah 64:8 (KJV)

God is the capable and intelligent potter, the wheel represents the procedure the potter will use, which represent everyday life situations, the plan is to center the clay, make sure all of the impurities are out of the clay, the potter will apply pressure on the clay add some water to keep it moist for pliability. Representing how we must be in the Master hands, because he is making a masterpiece (Ephesian 2:10 NLT) and a vessel of honor (2 Timothy 2:20, 21). The Potter has a specific purpose for the clay, and the potters needs the clay to cooperate, and be free from impurities.

"GOD told Jeremiah, "Up on your feet! Go to the potter's house. When you get there, I'll tell you what I have to say."3-4 So I went to the potter's house, and sure enough, the potter was there, working away at his wheel. Whenever the pot the potter was working on turned out badly, as sometimes happens when you are working with clay, the potter would simply start over and use the same clay to make another pot.5-10 Then GOD's Message came to me: "Can't I do just as this potter does, people of Israel?" GOD's Decree! "Watch this potter. In the same way that this Potter works his clay, I work on you, people of Israel. At any moment I may decide to pull up a people or a country by the roots and get rid of them. But if they repent of their wicked lives, I will think twice and start over with them. At another time I might decide to plant a people or country, but if they don't cooperate and won't listen to me, I will think again and give up on the plans I had for them." Jeremiah 18:1-10 (MSG)

The Making of a Woman

Answer Key

- **Bars**
  ... help you stretch and become more flexible, just like the way a dancer uses a barre.
- **Blocks**
  ... make it necessary to reposition yourself for a new start, in the same way that runners use blocks before they start a race.
- **Challenges**
  ... help you grow your knowledge, skills, experience and resources.
- **Checks**
  ... make you to rethink your options and actions, in the same way a check does in the game of chess.
- **Dampers**
  ... help you slow down and cool off, just like a fireplace damper.
- **Hurdles**
  ... require you to gain momentum so you can leap over them.
- **Impassable Obstacles**
  ... force you to find another way around them.
- **Impediments**
  ... help you to slow down and exercise caution in choosing your next steps.
- **Knots**
  ... make you stop and look carefully at the way things are connected, and then work patiently to loosen or cut through the binds within yourself or your environment.
- **Turnstiles**
  ... make you bid your time till things change.
- **Vices**
  ... put the pressure on and test whether we are strong enough to handle the consequences.
- **Walls**
  ... make you look around for a ladder or an overhanging tree you can climb. Or they can inspire you to build an earthen ramp so everyone can climb over them.

References

1. Arise and Shine

By CNN Staff (2015). Death Toll in Nepal earthquake tops 8,000. Retrieved August 17, 2015. From http://www.cnn.com/2015/05/10/asia/nepal-earthquake-death-toll/index.html

2. Two perspectives

Thinking One Can. The Wellspring for Young People, Pilgrim Press, Boston, Vol LXIII, no.42, October 20, 1906.
- reprinted in: Sharpe, Estelle Avery. 1910. Foundation Stones of Success, Vol I: Conversational Lessons on Social Ethics. Howard-Severance Co., Chicago, IL.

Yahoo! Image Search Results on Empowerment" Yahoo Images. World Wide Web June 20, 2015

3. Inspirational & Motivational tips

Ross. A. (2015). Harriet Tubman. Executive Summary. Retrieved July 9, 2015. From http://www.nndb.com/people/847/000031754/

4. Experiment

Alcom. R. ((2010). What Does Roman 8:28? Retrieved June 17, 2015. From http://www.epm.org/resources/2010/Mar/21/romans-828-what-does-it-really-mean/

5. Intro/Obstacle Quiz

Dowler.CA. (2015). Do You Know The Kinds of Life Obstacles? Retrieved April 25, 2015. From http://www.manifestyourpotential.com/life/make_sense_of_life/life_lessons_events/life_tasks/15_obstacles_in_life.htm

6. Definitions
All Definitions. (n.d.). In *Merriam Webster Online,* Retrieved September 24, 2014, from http://www.merriam-webster.com/dictionary/citation.

10. Helen Keller

Hermann, Dorothy, *Helen Keller. A Life*. Chicago: University of Chicago Press, 1999

The Making of a Woman

Keller, Helen. *The Story of My Life*. New York: Bantam Books, 1990

11. Rose Kennedy
    Rose Kennedy. (2015). The Biography.com website. Retrieved 05:14, Jul 11, 2015, from http://www.biography.com/people/rose-kennedy-9542623
12. Madam CJ Walker
    Madam C.J. Walker. (2015). The Biography.com website. Retrieved 05:18, Jul 11, 2015, from http://www.biography.com/people/madam-cj-walker-9522174.
13. Body Testimony 1
    Center for Disease Control Prevention. (2015). Women Health. Retrieved July 1, 2015. From http://www.cdc.gov/women/lcod/

    Rush University Medical Center. (ND). Is There One Trick to Loosing Belly Fat. Retrieved July 1, 2015. From https://www.rush.edu/health-wellness/discover-health/losing-belly-fat

Photos

Helen Keller page 45
   https://www.google.com/#q=public+domain+helen+keller+photos
Rose Kennedy page 51
   https://www.google.com/#q=public+domain+rose+kennedy+photos
Madam C. J Walker page 57
   https://www.google.com/#q=public+domain+madam+c+j+walker+photos
Tao Pochon page 62
   https://www.google.com/#q=public+domain+Tao+Porchon+photo
Lisa Nicholas page 70
   https://www.google.com/#q=public+domain+%09Lisa+Nicholas+photo
Joyce Myers page 77
   https://www.google.com/#q=public+domain+%09joyce+meyer++photo

www.ingramcontent.com/pod-product-compliance
Lightning Source LLC
Chambersburg PA
CBHW071513150426
43191CB00009B/1514